IMAGINE LIVING HERE

This Place Is

CROWDED

JAPAN

Vicki Cobb

Illustrations by
Barbara Lavallee

Walker and Company
New York

To the memory of Paula D. Wolf and Clarence H. Koehler

The author and illustrator gratefully acknowledge the help of the following people: Professor Koya Azumi, International Christian University; translator Chie Fujita; interpreter Chigusa Ogino; Momo Yuriko, Wakako Shimabukuro, Hiroshi Tsukahara, Toshiichi Uraki, Yoshikazu Iwasaki, our friends in Tokyo; Goodwill Guides Nick Y. Kurata (Tokyo), Keiko Kobayashi (western Kyoto), Yuri Ibuki (Kyoto), Haruko Okada (Kanazawa); agricultural rice expert Kunimi Kimura; Wendy Taniguchi, friend in Kyoto; and Grace Herget of the Japan National Tourist Organization.

Illustrations © 1992 by Barbara Lavallee

Copyright © 1992 by Vicki Cobb

First published in the United States of America in 1992
by Walker Publishing Company, Inc.

Published simultaneously in Canada by Thomas Allen & Son
Canada, Limited, Markham, Ontario

Library of Congress Cataloging-in-Publication Data
Cobb, Vicki.
This place is crowded / Vicki Cobb ; illustrated by Barbara
Lavallee.
p. cm. — (Imagine living here)
Summary: Describes transportation, education, home life, holidays,
and other aspects of life in the heavily populated island nation of
Japan.
ISBN 0-8027-8145-4 (trade). — ISBN 0-8027-8146-2 (rein)
1. Japan — Social life and customs — 1945– — Juvenile literature.
[1. Japan — Social life and customs.] I. Lavallee, Barbara, ill.
II. Title. III. Series: Cobb, Vicki. Imagine living here.
DS822.5.C63   1992
952.04 — dc20   91-15710
                                                                CIP
                                                                 AC

Printed in Hong Kong

2 4 6 8 10 9 7 5 3

If you went to school in Tokyo, Japan, you might travel on the subway during the morning rush hour. You would get on line behind a mark showing where the train doors will open. The train is so full of people that you think you will never squeeze in. But a man in a uniform and white gloves stands by the door and pushes you in. That is his job. Inside, you are packed so closely with others that you cannot move. Windows have been known to pop from the pressure of so many people. But the Japanese are calm and orderly in crowds. When it rains on busy Tokyo streets, people expertly raise and lower their umbrellas so they don't bump into one another. It's hard to find a place to spread your towel on a beach. Crowds are one thing you can count on in Japan.

Japan is a nation of about 121 million people living on four main islands and thousands of smaller islands. If half the people in the United States moved to Montana, it would be about as crowded. Three-quarters of Japan is covered with rugged, heavily wooded mountains. So most people live on a narrow strip of land along the Pacific coast of Honshu, the largest island.

If people were spread out evenly over the world, there would be 87 people in every square mile. If people were spread out evenly in Japan, there would be about 825 people in every square mile. In the populated areas in Japan, there are almost 5,000 people in each square mile. Between Tokyo and Yokohama there are more than 23,000 people in every square mile. Japan is crowded. But the Japanese don't mind overcrowding. In fact, they say that their most important product is people.

The mountainous islands of Japan lie on the Pacific Ring of Fire. This is a fault line under the Pacific Ocean where earthquakes and volcanic eruptions are common. One out of every ten of the world's volcanoes, both active and inactive, is in Japan. The most famous volcano is Mount Fuji, which last erupted in 1707. It rises more than 10,000 feet above sea level. Over half a million people climb it every year.

The hot earth that lies under volcanoes also produces hot springs. There are many spas in the Japanese mountains where people enjoy taking baths in natural hot water, which sometimes smells of sulfur. Natural hot water is pumped through small mountain villages to heat homes. In some places, where hot water collects in the ground or a basin, it is used to hard boil eggs.

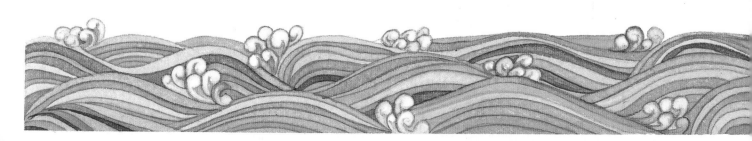

The Japanese have a legend that says a giant fish sleeps under their islands. Earthquakes are caused when the fish awakens and flicks its tail. The last major earthquake in Tokyo was in 1923 and killed 130,000 people. Scientists think that major earthquakes occur about every 60 years, so Japan is overdue for another one. The modern skyscrapers of the major cities are specially designed to wave back and forth during an earthquake without collapsing.

There is very little land that is good for farming. Every patch that can be farmed has crops growing on it. About half of the farmland is used to grow rice.

Rice is a kind of grass that once grew wild in swamps. Cultivated rice needs a lot of water. The rice fields or paddies must be flooded when the rice seedlings are planted by the farmer. Once, the backbreaking work of planting seedlings was done by hand. But today's rice farmers have special tractors with wheels that ride well in mud. They automatically plant seedlings in neat rows.

The problem that faced early rice farmers was how to get water to the fields. Fortunately, there was plenty of water for everyone. Instead of competing for water, farmers joined together and worked as teams to build irrigation ditches that would flood everyone's paddies. The teamwork that came from early rice farmers has carried over into modern Japanese life. The Japanese know how to cooperate and work together to get things done.

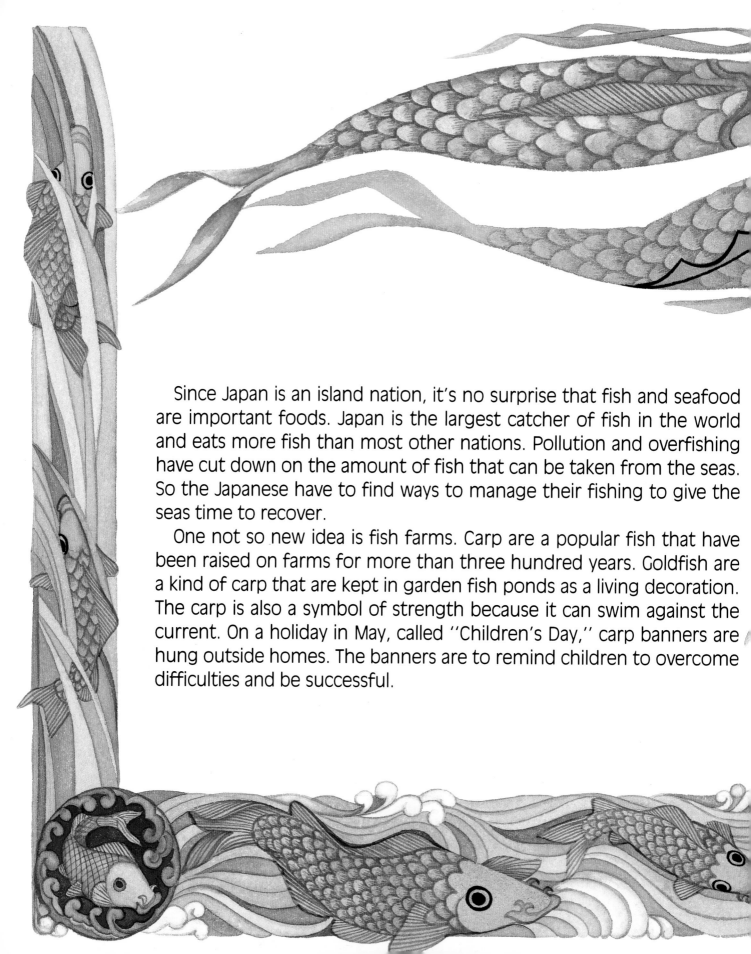

Since Japan is an island nation, it's no surprise that fish and seafood are important foods. Japan is the largest catcher of fish in the world and eats more fish than most other nations. Pollution and overfishing have cut down on the amount of fish that can be taken from the seas. So the Japanese have to find ways to manage their fishing to give the seas time to recover.

One not so new idea is fish farms. Carp are a popular fish that have been raised on farms for more than three hundred years. Goldfish are a kind of carp that are kept in garden fish ponds as a living decoration. The carp is also a symbol of strength because it can swim against the current. On a holiday in May, called "Children's Day," carp banners are hung outside homes. The banners are to remind children to overcome difficulties and be successful.

Most of the fish eaten by the 11 million Tokyo residents arrive each day at a huge central market. At five o'clock every morning, at least 100 different kinds of fish and seafood are auctioned to the middlemen who will sell the fish to local stores and restaurants. The fish arrive in Styrofoam crates. Outside the market are huge ovens that burn the piles of used packing crates.

Most Japanese shop every day for food. Freshness is one reason, but another is that most Japanese homes don't have large freezers or a lot of storage space. Raw fish, called sashimi, is a popular favorite, but only fresh fish is good to eat raw. In addition to fish and rice, the Japanese eat seaweed, tofu (a cheeselike food made from soybeans), noodles, and many different kinds of pickled vegetables. Japanese food is cut up and arranged in the kitchen so you don't need a knife at the dinner table. All you need are chopsticks. It is important that the food look beautiful as well as taste delicious. Most restaurants have plastic or wax models of their different dishes on display. That way, you can pick what you want to eat just by pointing.

Since land is scarce, Japanese houses are usually much smaller than American houses. There is not much furniture. Most of the rooms have a floor covering of mats made out of straw called tatami. Tatami is comfortable to sit on and helps keep the room warm in winter. Since the Japanese always take off their shoes before entering a home, the tatami mats don't get worn or dirty quickly. People sit on cushions on the floor and eat at low tables. At night, they sleep on mattresses on the floor. During the day the bedding is folded away in closets.

The Japanese home has a peaceful, simple style that is a welcome relief from the busy world outside. The preparing and drinking of green tea is an ordered, soothing ceremony. The aim of the Tea Ceremony is to prepare and serve green tea so politely and simply that everyone experiences feelings of calmness and peace of mind. Wealthy people sometimes have separate teahouses just for this ceremony. Others have a plain, spotlessly clean room with only tatami mats on the floor and perhaps a single flower or branch for decoration.

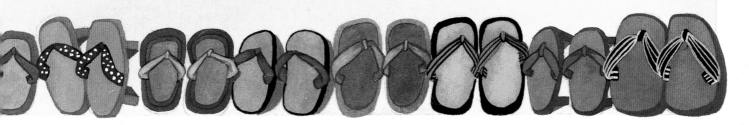

The Japanese live so closely together that they have developed strict rules for good manners. Even within a family people are considerate of one another. When two people meet they don't kiss or shake hands. Instead they bow to each other. One way of showing respect is to bow very deeply. People have a very clear understanding of how a person is supposed to behave depending on his or her role. The idea is to keep things as peaceful and harmonious as possible. Even when people disagree, they try to settle their problems calmly. Their arguments may seem very formal and stiff to an outsider. There is very little violent fighting in Japan and the streets of Japanese cities are safe and crime free.

Manners and politeness are part of the martial arts and the national sport of sumo wrestling. In a sumo bout, two huge wrestlers lunge at each other, each trying to force the other out of a ring outlined on a hard-packed clay floor. A sumo bout lasts only about 30 seconds, although ceremonies before and after last much longer.

Before the start of each day's training, sumo wrestlers recite their belief: ''Sumo begins and ends with courtesy, not only in the ring but in life.'' In spite of their weight, which ranges from about 220 pounds to more than 500, sumo wrestlers are extremely strong, very fit, and flexible enough to do splits. They wear a 30-foot-long belt artfully wrapped around their waists and between their legs. A sumo wrestler automatically loses the bout if his belt falls off.

The value that the Japanese place on order and their love of nature is celebrated in their gardens. Every plant is planned by gardeners to please the eye but look as natural as possible. The branches of trees are trained to grow the way gardeners think nature ideally intended. Some gardens have only a few carefully placed rocks that are surrounded by sand that has been raked in a pattern. Stone lanterns highlight the important parts of a garden.

Japanese cherry trees are famous all over the world. The Japanese have made gifts of cherry trees to many nations. In the spring, people have parties to enjoy the cherry blossoms, which stand for beauty and the shortness of life, since the blossoms only last a few days.

Another famous Japanese plant is bamboo. Bamboo is a woody kind of grass that is used to make everything from pipes to furniture to musical instruments. It can grow very quickly, as much as three feet a day. Bamboo trees are a symbol of loyalty because they are so strong and sturdy, but the flowers are considered unlucky. Once a bamboo tree flowers, it dies.

Throughout the history of Japan, powerful people were rewarded with gifts of land. The landowners ruled over the people who worked their land. The rulers built elaborate palaces for themselves with spacious rooms and acres of gardens. They spared no expense. In Kyoto, which was the capital of Japan for more than a thousand years, the famous Golden Pavilion is completely covered with gold foil. It was built in 1393 by a military ruler, a shogun, as a retirement home. The pavilion is at the edge of a lake that reflects its golden image, one of wealth and peace. After his father's death, the shogun's son changed the house into a temple. When it was burned to the ground in 1950, it was rebuilt five years later exactly as originally planned.

Another powerful shogun of Kyoto, who wanted a house finer than that of the emperor, built his castle in 1603. The huge inside rooms were decorated with the finest art. The shogun sat on a raised throne to greet his guests. But he was clearly afraid of his enemies. Each building of his palace had a secret room where bodyguards kept watch. The rooms the shogun used locked only from the inside. The outside hallways had special floors that chirped like birds when they were stepped on to warn against unwanted intruders.

Today, the old system of ruling by land ownership no longer exists. Japan is a democracy. The capital is Tokyo. Most of the temples and palaces are public museums and parks.

When you visit museums, castles, temples, and parks in Japan you see groups of schoolchildren everywhere. Often they are wearing school uniforms or school caps. Education is very important to the Japanese and includes many school trips to historic places. Children go to school five and a half days a week all year long except for a six-week vacation in the summer, two weeks around New Year's Day, and two weeks in the spring. Homework is given every night starting in first grade. About half the children get extra help by going to a private school after their regular school day. It is called a *juku*, meaning "cram school." There they also get special lessons in arts like music, painting, and calligraphy, which is a fancy kind of handwriting.

Japanese children are encouraged to be happiest as a part of a group. They are discouraged from acting independently and from original thinking. If a child stands out from the rest, he or she will be ignored by the others. The Japanese have a saying that expresses this thinking: "The nail that sticks up will be hammered down." Some foreign children attend Japanese schools, but they are never fully accepted by the Japanese children. The Japanese feel a special pride in being Japanese. The word *gaijin* (guy-jin) is used to describe all outsiders or non-Japanese.

Children must go to school until they finish high school. The last year of high school is spent getting ready to take an exam that decides who can enter the best universities. The pressure to do well is enormous. The children who don't make it and their families suffer painful feelings of failure.

The values of education, hard work, self-discipline, teamwork, and obedience have brought success to Japanese industry. Just as school is the center of children's lives, the company is the center for working adults.

Many men and some women, particularly if they have jobs with a lot of responsibility, work more than sixty hours a week. Since many of them travel at least two hours to get to work, they would get home just in time to start back to work again. So they rent a tiny "sleeping capsule," a space just big enough to sleep in.

Most workers stay with the same company for life. All the workers, not just the bosses, help decide how to make their products better. Japanese cars, televisions, stereos, and cameras are among the finest you can buy and they are sold all over the world. Since World War II, Japan has become one of the wealthiest nations in the world.

The Japanese are known for taking ideas developed and invented by people in other countries and improving them. They have been particularly successful with high-tech products. A super-sharp television, amazing household robots, and a computerized player-piano that reproduces the same notes on a keyboard exactly as struck by a concert pianist are a few of the ideas they are working on.

In order to move its millions of people the Japanese have built one of the best railroad systems in the world. All of the cities and towns are linked by railroads. The major cities, such as Tokyo and Osaka, have a superexpress train that travels at 130 miles per hour. It's called the "bullet train" because of its streamlined shape and high speed.

The Japanese are developing a train that will carry passengers at a speed of 310 miles per hour. This train will not have wheels. In fact, it won't even touch the tracks while it's moving. It will "float" noiselessly above the tracks as it moves along, propelled by superstrong magnets.

You can't own a car in Japan unless you can prove that you have a place to park it. Nevertheless, two out of three households have a car. Like most modern countries, Japan has a good system of roads and highways.

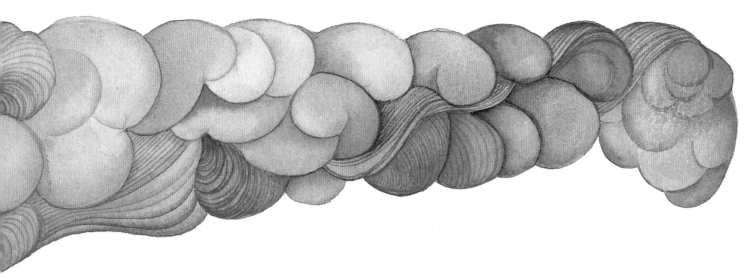

In order for trains and cars to get from one island to another, Japan has built some amazing bridges and tunnels. The mile-long bridge across part of the Inland Sea between Honshu, the main island, and Shikoku is the longest suspension bridge in Asia. A 33½-mile tunnel has been built between Honshu and the northern island of Hokkaido. It is the longest tunnel in the world and it took more than fifteen years to build.

Pollution is the price of a crowded industrial civilization. In the 1960s air pollution became a serious problem for the Japanese. Many people became ill from the poor air quality. This led to the formation of the Environment Agency. Strict laws were passed to cut down harmful automobile fumes. Factories have to clean up the waste that comes out of their smokestacks. These laws have worked fairly well and air pollution is not the problem it once was. But water pollution is still a problem in many places.

Another problem is garbage. The best use of garbage has been landfill, particularly along the coast. This creates much-needed space where none existed. A park in Tokyo is built on garbage landfill. Recycling paper, glass, and aluminum cans are some of the ways to handle some of the trash. Japan recycles almost half of its waste paper—more than any other country. It also recycles slightly more than half its bottles and four out of ten aluminum cans. Soda-can crushers were recently installed on Mount Fuji. Park officials figured that a crushed can would be more likely to be back-packed off the mountain than left behind on the trail.

The Japanese have many holidays and festivals throughout the year. Some of the most popular, like the spring and fall festivals in Takayama in the Japan Alps, draw crowds from all over Japan. They jam the streets to watch the gorgeous floats that parade through the city streets. Festivals show off the art, music, and traditions of people who work and play well together. Can you imagine living here?